HANDMADE LOVE

T0303688

HANDMADE LOVE

JULIE R. ENSZER

BODY LANGUAGE 05

A MIDSUMMER NIGHT'S PRESS

New York

for Kim, with love

A Midsummer Night's Press
16 West 36th Street
2nd Floor
New York, NY 10018
amidsummernightspress@gmail.com
www.amidsummernightspress.com

Grateful acknowledgement is given to the editors of the following publications in which many of these poems first appeared (sometimes in a different form): *A-pos-tro-phe*: "In My Fantasy Single Life"; *billet-doux: an Anthology* (Dancing Girl Press): "Dear Donald"; *Del Sol Review*: "You Are Not Like Them"; *Glass: A Journal of Poetry*: "Jade Ring"; *Harrington Lesbian Fiction Quarterly*: "Morning Pant" & "If"; *OCHO*: "Seeing Annie Liebovitz's *A Photographer's Life* 1990-2005" & "Cunts"; *On the Issues Magazine*: "Absolutely No Car Repairs in the Parking Lot"; *Poetry Fish*: "First Kiss"; *Poemeleon*: "Conceptual Sex"; *Room of One's Own*: "When We Were Feminists"; *Salt River Review*: "When Grace Got Married"; *So to Speak*: "Absolutely No Car Repairs in the Parking Lot"; *Suspect Thoughts*: "Stroke" & "Terms of Endearment"; *Technodyke.com*: "Handmade Love"; *Windy City Times Pride Literary Supplements*: "Constantin Brancusi's The Kiss" & "Making Love After Many Years"

Gratitude to my teachers, most particularly Stanley Plumly who plucked me from despair and changed my life completely, also Michael Collier, Martha Nell Smith, Robin Becker, and Minnie Bruce Pratt. Thank you to my friends and first readers, Steffan DeClue, Sally Rosen Kindred, Carrie Russell, and Merry Gangemi. Appreciation to Lawrence Schimel for his work as an editor and publisher— besos! Finally, my most beloved one; words are not enough, but they are all I have. Thank you for your companionship and unending commitment, as well as for the Millender Center, the first Mac laptop, reminding me that I'm no Andrea Dworkin, and for continuing still to believe in me.

NOTES: "My Fantasy Single Life": "hooning" is an Australian colloquialism for behaving recklessly. "Constantin Brancusi's *The Kiss*": The line "Love should be put into action" is from Elizabeth Bishop's poem "Chemin de Fer." "Was Elizabeth Bishop a Lesbian?": "lifting belly" and "rose is a rose is a rose" are both from poems by Gertrude Stein.

Designed by Marróndediseño www.quintatinta.com
Upper cover photo © Mili Hernández. Reprinted by permission.

First edition, April 2010.

ISBN-13: 978-0-9794208-5-6
ISBN-10: 0-9794208-5-7

Printed in Spain.

CONTENTS

WHEN WE WERE FEMINISTS

> *"I love you more than I did when you were mine."*
> —*Prince*

When we were feminists, feminism was like cooking the first meal
After grocery shopping. You know:
When all of the vegetables have the patina of freshness,
When the fruit feels firm, even weighty, in your hand,
When the knife slides through perfectly from the right
       combination of resistance and forgiveness.

When you cook with the leisure of a weekend.

Now feminism is like the meal you make five days after shopping,
When you are exhausted from working all day,
When you try to perk up wilted red and green leaf lettuce in a
       bath of cold water,
When you coax leftovers with salt and spices to make them
       seem new and somehow, fresh.

When you cook simply because you have to eat.

When we were feminists, we spent Saturday mornings at
      women's clinics.

After contracepting Friday night, we hoped only to see the
      outside

Where anti-abortion protesters harassed women seeking
      health care,

Where angry, white men pulled at our coats and earring,
      shouting, "Lesbian."

Where pious, white women prayed for our souls and sang
      hymns.

Where we sought to preserve a basic right: self-determination.

Now we spend Saturday mornings walking our dogs and
      eating brunch,

Sometimes with friends, at restaurants, where they recount
      their stories of hyper-conception,

Where they tell us detailed anecdotes of unnatural (donor)
      selection,

Where they describe the speculum of impregnation,

Where they seek to ensure yet another right: self-perpetuation.

When we were feminists, we planned for equality in our
      relationships,

Like we planned to have clean houses with walls of orderly books:

Because it was aesthetically and emotionally pleasing,

Because we believed in it, because we could, because it was our
        dream,

Because we lived in small spaces; because our relationships
        were without demonstrated endurance.

Now equality in our relationship is piled in the corner next to a
        stack of books all covered
With a thick layer of dust and surrounded by floating globules
        of dog and cat hair.
Because we don't have time to clean.
Because we are caught in the interstices of disagreements,
        escalating to arguments,
Because we are caught in the fissures of human, intimate
        relationships,
Because we navigate, on a daily basis, notions of equality,
        sometimes painfully, sometimes tediously,
Because we wonder, "Am I really equal if I pick up your dry
        cleaning?"
Because feminism taunts us with principles, economics, love,
        equality and companionship at odds often
Though, sometimes, briefly, for a few, luminous moments, at
        evens.

Because we live in large houses; because our relationships are
        our promise to the future.

When we were feminists, we espoused equal pay for equal work
With clarity of uncomplicated youth and the certainty of truth.
Although, in honest groups of feminist women only, sometimes
    we wondered:
Will we break through the glass ceiling? Do we want to?
Will we serve equally in the military? Do we want to?
Will we ever elect a woman to be President? Do we want to?

Will it all come out equal in the end? We know: it won't. Do we
    want it to?

Now we work every day and sometimes earn more than our
    male counterparts, and sometimes less,
And sometimes there is parity even though we have more
    education and experience,
And sometimes we just don't know or can't ask or couldn't
    really determine.
And sometimes we are just thankful for work and a paycheck.
And sometimes we are not. And sometimes, we wonder:

At the end of the day, does it matter? Will I be any happier? We
    know: we don't know.

When we were feminists, we made impromptu picnics in the
    park.
A single book and ten dollars worth of groceries would satisfy
    for an afternoon.

French cheeses, fresh fruit, crackers, and a bottle of cheap wine.
All served at room temperature as we sat on the naked grass.

When we were feminists, we made impromptu picnics in the
        park.

Now, I can rarely find an afternoon to read. I cannot remember
        the last trip to the grocery store
When I spent less than ten dollars. The other day, I made baked
        brie with grapes
Scavenged from the fruit and vegetable crisper. I cannot
        remember when I bought them.
They were not bad exactly—slightly wilted and becoming
        dehydrated.
(In fact, it was like the mystery of raisins was being revealed in
        their puckering skins.)

Even without the pop from the taut skins of fresh grapes,
Without the spray of fresh juice in my mouth, it was good.
And I sat on my bed. And I read a book. It was good like
Picking up a copy of Ms. Magazine at the train station.
I remember how feminism first tasted in my mouth.

I remember impromptu picnics in the park. I remember when
        we were feminists.

I

FIRST KISS

Late at night in the Michigan woods,
we would creep out of our cabin, walk
onto the dock, zip our sleeping bags

together. Under the stars, we talked
while the lake lapped
rotting legs of the dock.

11 p.m. Midnight. Words
carried us into the next day.
Our teenaged bodies shrouded

in shorts and t-shirts,
we laughed, shared stories and secrets
in our docked double bed.

I wanted to kiss you.
I always waited late
into the night thinking,

could I pretend it was just an accident?
Lay my lips on yours: mid-sentence,
mid-giggle, mid-teenage confession.

Could I pretend? Could I pretend?
We woke at sunrise;
light piercing our eyes.

We unzipped our bed
and skulked back to the cabin
to awaken alone again.

YOU ARE NOT LIKE THEM

mother speaks these words
with punishing derision

you do not just go to work
take care of the dogs
mow the lawn

you're filthy lesbians
you are not like them

but what if we were?
what if we were exactly like them?

my best friend Michael
fears this
all the homos living in the suburbs

working
gardening
tending to the neighborhood

he visits our home
he says he likes it

but he tells me

urgently
defiantly
he tells me

you are not like them

CONCEPTUAL SEX

For Sally

I've never had it
unless you count fantasies:
I conceptualized another woman
and touched myself
before I ever had sex,
but sex to conceive?
I can't comprehend
the concept.
Forgive me,
you're copulating
crazily sans contraception.
It is your mission
in the missionary position
to create the conditions
for insemination,
to stimulate fertilization,
ultimately to commence
gestation; all in all
we might colloquially
call such a collection
of extracurriculars "getting
knocked up"—an elementary

enterprise which was less work
with more excitement
when we were teens
conceptualizing sex.

MORNING PANT

I know what women want to eat in the morning.
On Sunday, in college, I would cook eggs,
scrambled or fried, potatoes, and bacon—
pork then was still a subversion. Breakfast

for my best friend and the man she slept with last night.
I knew what women wanted to eat in the morning.
Alone on Saturday, I found ways to feed them on Sunday: eggs,
scrambled or fried, potatoes, and bacon.

The prospect of seducing a woman seemed simple, but
my best friend seduced the man she slept with last night
leaving my bed empty, my hands idle, my lips
alone on Saturday, until I found ways to feed them on Sunday.

Sauces can satisfy the need to break from the mundane.
The prospect of seducing a woman seems simple:
wine, marinara arrabiata, raspberry coulis. Delicious dinner still
left my bed empty, my hands idle, my lips

dry. I could only imagine the shimmer of gloss
sauce. Satisfy the need to break from the mundane
on my lips: a wax or paraffin base, Vaseline in a pinch.

Franzia, tomato sauce, berry puree—a delicious dinner still,

but I imagined more—a peak that would not leave my pussy
dry. I could imagine only the shimmer of gloss
from a woman's juices on my chin after licking and licking
her lips. No wax or paraffin. (Third) base; Vaseline; a pinch.

Then I met a woman one Sunday, in college.
Finally I had more—a peak that left my pussy
weary but satisfied. After rest she begged for more:
I know what women want to eat in the morning.

JADE RING

A large oblong stone,
set in silver or white gold,
perfectly smooth and commanding
on the real estate of her hand.
I want a woman with jade.

Her fingers confidently adorned
with a single, bold stone,
worn, unselfconsciously,

on the middle finger of her hand.
I imagine warming it's cool exterior
with my wetness below. It's hard frame
pressing my strong muscles.

I'd like your jade ring
to leave its imprint between my legs.

IF

If you were a man
and I was straight
we could get married

today in all fifty states.
Just a few requirements
to demonstrate:

age, blood test, cash payment.
Give money, give blood
(a small investment)

to be wed.
Before Massachusetts there were no options for us queers.
Straight people could

live together five or seven years—
state by state it varies—
common law marriage governments revere.

With only time, we could be married;
that is, if you were a man and I was straight.
Then if you died,

suddenly, intestate,
I'd be protected, even affirmed,
by the law. Can you relate?

No. You're not a man—
thank G-d—and I'm not
straight. We can

not tie the knot.
(Besides such legitimacy might make
lesbianism a little less hot.)

HIBISCUS

This summer, I saw it.
A bloom so large, it drew me in.
Five petals point, bud, then open
like fingers. I am riveted; I want
to slide inside: sleep next to the stamen,
let the pistil tickle my nipples.
At rest, this seed takes root:
I know why men hate women.

At the end of August, when the creek
near my house was bone dry, the river bed perforated,
I saw another. Uncultivated, surviving drought,
papery petals delicate, yet still filled with power.
With her parched voice,
the white hibiscus whispered,
these are the women to fear most:
the ones that grow wild by the river.

SEEING ANNIE LIEBOVITZ'S *A PHOTOGRAPHER'S LIFE 1990-2006*

When I walk in already I am angry
about Susan "the long-term friend."
Another for whom the study of gay men,
fashionable, but pussy-licking lesbians
are to be denied. Even the obituary
reads only, *she is survived by a son
and a sister.* Three years later,
Annie concedes, *Yes, you could say we were
Lesbians, though it is not a word Susan
would use*—and here she pauses, *or approve.*
So when I see Susan in the small photos,
snapshots amid outsized glitz and posed glamour
enlarged to be bigger than any one life,
she peers out at me as if from a small
cabinet or cupboard, cramped,
not even large enough to be a closet.
Annie pins these pictures in a barn,
listening to Rosanne Cash, crying. She lives on.
I soften to Susan. Her cancer-wizened face,
shaved head, tired eyes. I want her bookshelves,
filled and ordered. I want her trip to France and Jordan,
but most of all, I want her to use my words,
which now she will never do.

DEAR DONALD,

Your poems about sex embarrass me.
I'd like the erotic to be my realm: womanly, queer.
Yet there you are, an old man, writing desire,
fornicating with a younger woman. Though
that is inaccurate: you married her. Perhaps once
I would have been offended, but that would have been bluster
to cover embarrassment. In youth, sex seems
to be the domain of the young. Of course, it isn't.

Now, I have more investment in sex as an older person,
becoming one myself, though, I hasten to add, not nearly
as old as you. Forgive me if that offends. Advancing age
has me imagining myself in my sixties, and, like you,
having sex in the afternoons. It is deeply pleasurable and erotic;
so much so, I don't even think of you.

IN MY FANTASY SINGLE LIFE

I am hooning[1] around
with lots and lots of women
because for some unknown,
yet incredible, reason,
I am able to stay awake passed 10:30 p.m.,
and I am not spending that time
watching TV and figuring out the conclusions
to all my favorite shows,
which I have missed in my real married life
when I fall asleep before 10:30 p.m.,
oh no, I am hanging out at bars and clubs
and other hip places where hot lesbians
are gathered, and I am flirting
and I am dancing and I am seducing
hot women and eating their pussies
in bathrooms or my car or my hip
fantasy single life city condo

and I like it and I want it
to continue (who wouldn't?)
until one night this really fine woman
is fucking me really good and really hard
and just as I am about to come, she says

I love you (who says that in someone
else's fantasy?) and I have to stop and say
No, you don't love me
this is sex not love and
I say it firmly and I mean it
because all of a sudden
I remember this is my fantasy single life—
where I have wild sex without love—
but I live in reality somewhere and there,
in that reality, there I remember: I know love.

HANDMADE LOVE

In kindergarten, I carried a schoolbag
my mother made from fabric with fairy tale scenes.

For three years, it was my most prized possession.
When I was scared, I would look at the bag and recite

fairy tales to myself. Goldilocks, Little Red Riding Hood,
the Golden Swan. These girls faced fear and survived.

In my carefully buttoned bag, I carried books, rocks, pencils,
and other childhood treasures. At seven, teased by children

for my handmade bag and matching dress, I demanded
store bought clothes, a back pack. Now my briefcase

is leather and bulging with files, but I yearn for my childhood bag
still in my closet. Sometimes when I am alone

I pull it out and carry it around the house filled with special
                    objects:
papers, pens, stones, and books, items not so different

from when I was a child. I value handmade things.
I believe that there are two kinds of love in this world:

inherited and handmade. Yes, we inherit love
but my people, my people make love by hand.

CONSTANTIN BRANCUSI'S *THE KISS*

is small and compact and made from limestone.
It sits on a rough wood platform—like a railroad tie—
that makes me think of the road of iron,
and the dirty hermit screaming
Love should be put into action.
The easy embrace of these two lovers:
the way their arms fit perfectly
around the other
the same height
their lips and eyes meet exactly
the way their hair falls similarly down their face.
Isn't that what we all want in a lover?
The perfect match.
The perfect moment.
This is what I despise about poems—
they way they isolate
distill life to only the good parts
they never capture this—
harsh words in morning or constipation or warts.
We save these for television commercials
though now even those seem optional
as though if we wish
we could look away from our need

for hemorrhoidal creams, shady lawyers,
and breakfast cereals fortified with fiber—
this is the way of the modern world:
take away, take away, take away.
Until we realize too much has been removed
and now must be replaced, frantically, inadequately
like on the train this morning when I remembered
not what I had forgotten
but what I had missed—
earlier, in anger, our goodbye kiss.

II

ABSOLUTELY NO CAR REPAIRS
IN THE PARKING LOT

Three people are working on old, American cars.
One man with a white van—his mobile mechanic's shop—
has pulled the engine out of a black Monte Carlo.
Another crawls from under a Sunbird
rusted and battered tail pipe in hand.
The third, an Escort, hood open, unattended.
Owners ostensibly inside the auto supply
searching for the proper replacement part.

Although I don't need one, I've brought a man.
Newly minted. Nine months ago, breasts removed—
scars from the surgical drains healed quickly
now the only skin rupture from needles
delivering daily hormones he refers to as T,
and the resulting faux-adolescent acne pimpling his face.
He's more of a man than me. Still, it takes us two tries
with a return in between to find wiper blades that fit.

I GIVE YOU A DIAMOND
RING AT THE AIRPORT

Because I cannot remember
all our special dinners
birthdays, anniversaries,
milestones—large and small—
I don't want a special
night to give you this ring.

I want it to be ordinary;
the way the ring would be
a part of your daily life—
a simple band, five diamonds—
first thing on each morning,
last thing off at night.

Ordinary even as it sits
on public display—
an announcement of fealty,
not quite matrimony,
or connubial bliss, but
some sort of commitment.

This is why I don't care when
the man sitting next to you—

middle aged, white, traveling
on business—walks away
when you say yes. When we
kiss. When we seal this covenant.

WHEN GRACE GOT MARRIED

Even in reruns, I cry during the episode
where Grace gets married. Tears first for Will, abandoned,
still hoping the friendship would not implode.

In twenty-two minutes, Grace, with the perfect companion,
leaves Will, suddenly another thirty-something has been,
the proverbial New York SGM with a married best friend.

Then, I cry, angry with Grace for finding the perfect husband
—a nice Jewish doctor. She invoked her privilege, embraced
a white dress, chuppah. Her left hand flaunts a wedding band.

I cry for myself as well. Will and Grace
struggled valiantly with the same notions of friendship
we did. They wanted to create a relational space

outside the sexually coupled world. Friendship
that primarily nurtured and sustained.
No words to describe the unlikely partnership,

but ample support, chaste affection, retained
sexuality. Unwittingly, they challenged us to consider:
can a primary relationship be maintained

without sex? Even after my own disaster,
I watched that show and I believed, yes, I believed.
Where you and I failed, Lis, what we cast asunder,

I watched with rapt attention, almost relieved,
dreaming of the possibility of familial success for Will
and Grace. Was it so impossible to conceive

of idealized friendship surviving still?
I rooted for them against all logic, against all reason.
Then Grace got married. I wept. It made me ill.

It didn't work for them either, after just five seasons.
Perhaps it cannot. Perhaps it never will. Perhaps our innate
biological being compels us to couple, demands

that we find a spiritual, emotional, and sexual mate.
I don't know. All I know is Grace got married.
So, Will better get out there and date.

Now that Grace is married, there will come a time,
if not sooner than later, when Grace won't even
respond to Will's email, just as you don't respond to mine.

STROKE

Dear Michael, The only strokes I wish
to hear of are the ones that happen

in your Jacuzzi during Saturday afternoon
seductions. When you and the beloved

fill the tub and suck and fuck,
then accidentally hit the plug.

Water drops below the jets.
Air shoots out. Mimics

sperm and semen from your cock.
Oh, yes. The only strokes I wish to

hear of are the ones that lead
inexorably to orgasm. Understand?

The only strokes I ever imagined
for you were in backrooms of bars or

on your giant king size bed in the loft
of your fussy Victorian home.

I never imagined you stroking clothed.
Sitting on a couch. Reading. No man

in sight or mind. Let me be clear:
I never expect you to leave me behind.

Perhaps it should have been evident.
Someday you, with more than twenty

years on me, would become sick.
Is this the ultimate consequence

of considering you my friend,
often with the adjective 'best?'

You survived the plague. Now
how can one weak vessel erase that?

Let me make it plain: I never expect
to let you go. I refuse and you must too.

Here is my imagined future:
visiting you at eighty, grumpy

and sarcastic. I give you a bear hug,
then a gentle stroke on your behind.

TERMS OF ENDEARMENT

For Liz

I mistakenly called you "missy"—
an inappropriate term of endearment for
a butch lesbian, the identity I assumed

you to have with your cropped hair, hip-riding
jeans and top buttoned down. Let me confess:
I assumed your identity for my own purposes.

I have an entire fantasy about your body and
what I could do with it based on you being
lesbian and butch. Then I learned you consider

yourself to be male—transgendered.
Yes, "missie" seems inappropriate.
Yet without diminuitive feminizations

I am left with few options to coo affection.
Immediately, I'd like to say "FTM trannie" and cast
upon you my feminine wiles, but can I?

I try Buddy? Pal? You chide me not to stoop to
Bubba. I won't. Still, all the phrases I think to utter
with cloying appreciation are wildly sexual—

How's it hanging? If I, an avowed fem lesbo,
flirt with you, now a man but still in a woman's body
(and, of course, with a woman lover),

Am I still gay? Or just queer? And if I don't
stoop, linguistically, that is,
but I would like to be on my knees and

have you fuck me from behind with a
big purple strap on like my wife does,
am I a homo? I just want to find

a word to address you and imbue it with affection.
I want to respect your gender identity and not reconsider
my own sexual orientation and erotic predilections.

That is probably too much to ask, which is why
my pussy is wet, my tongue is tied, and only my mind
has been fucked. Understand gender? Good luck.

FURTHER EVIDENCE

I am seeking further evidence of feminism in the new
        millennium.
It began with an alleged pimple in my hoo-hoo that grew and
        grew. I feared
only dirty women and hoes have unknown growths on their
        pussies.

Sunday night, unable to sit, in pain, I page my gynecologist.
        After explaining
what my wife has done to help, the on-call, nurse-midwife asks
        if I am pregnant.
I am seeking further evidence of feminism in the new
        millennium.

She recovers from my angry tirade with sound advice: sit in a
        hot tub, keep it clean,
apply hot compresses—it will form a head; the infection will
        expel. I still feel like
only dirty women and hoes have unknown growths on their
        pussies.

Three days later, I visit my gynecologist for our yearly smear.
>> She looks, grimaces, and
gives it a diagnostic name. Then suddenly, squeezes what
>> remains. More pain.
I am seeking further evidence of feminism in the new
>> millennium.

Afraid it will reappear, I search web sites on women's health for
>> "sebaceous vulval cyst,"
And am informed extra attention to hygiene will help in
>> prevention. Apparently,
only dirty women and hoes have unknown growths on their
>> pussies.

Then today—AHA—new evidence of feminism! A middle-aged,
>> balding, Asian man
sits on the Metro. His turquoise t-shirt proclaims: This is what a
>> radical feminist looks like.
I am seeking further evidence of feminism in the new
>> millennium.
Only dirty women and hoes have unknown growths on their
>> pussies.

COUPLETS FOR JEFF

For Jeff Colby, 1965-2007

For years, my friend Jeff was, unofficially, Detroit's gay mayor;
he'd staff every table, smile and shake; this was the role he
    savored.

There were jokes, polite guffaws, about his likeness to Rush
    Limbaugh—
it was uncanny—but his personal tastes ran more to Rimbaud.

Once I babysat for his cat. She escaped. Through a window. I
    lost her.
Two weeks later, thinking she'd been found. I called Jeff. He
    rushed over.

Scrawny, battered. The cat jumped into his arms. *This isn't Stimpy,*
he said, plaintively. *She wouldn't do that. She hated me.*

Besides, now I like being alone. Without cat responsibilities.
By then I had named her, Eponine. I'd just read *Les Miserables.*

My neighbors adopted the dear, though they called her Vivian.
Jeff lived his days with no paramour, not even a feline companion.

Last week, at forty-two, Jeff died in his sleep. The obituary notes
his historic, West Village home, (nothing more than a coded gay
      trope)
his boss's paean to his public service, his mother's mention of
      some
website where he was the greeter. With that, his life summary
      was done.

But I—I can't imagine him dying alone. Asleep? That's for old
      people
with blue hair whose murmurs at funerals are full of treacle.

No, I imagine him having wild, kinky sex. Dying mid-orgasm
with some little twinkie, who, though frightened by the final—
      nay fatal—spasms,

stayed long enough to roll him on his back, close his mouth, tuck
      him in
to be found by his mother when she came for brunch the next
      morning.

Yes, Jeff, this is how I remember you, fucking to the death.
It makes me less bereft, when I acknowledge, as I must, you've left.

SWAGGER

This youngish butch has the swagger
of just having taken a new lover.

I recognize it—the pose, the attitude—
from butches who have taken me.

I have placed my hands, my lips
on their breasts and spread their legs

as Moses parted the Red Sea.
I have given women this look,

this sense of satisfaction. Sexual,
yes, but sensual, emotional.

With my lips but with no words,
I have told them, *in this world,*

there is room for you. Be as you are.
Though my friend is young,

the swagger is not only their domain.
One of my lovers was exactly twice my age.

She had this self-certain look,
this smile. She exuded

the same happiness and satisfaction
as the young butch before me.

It is not a posture of youth,
though youth wears it well.

Even the wisdom of age cannot
suppress the delicious saunter

that is the exclusive province
of butch women. I celebrate

my friend's swagger, her joy
at new sex. She mourns,

as she must, how trapped
I am in my relationship, but

I've learned the swagger
is not only from a new lover.

This morning, after we made love
last night with a passion

that couldn't be quenched
and only stopped when the desire

to come again was overwhelmed
by the body's need for sleep,

my wife dressed in the dark and
left while I slept, though

I woke long enough to see
her perfect swagger.

THROUGH THE FLOWER

Until this morning, I had only seen it on the cover of her
      autobiography—
my preferred reading about artists and activists (I'm interested
      in people's lives)—
so when I saw it hanging on the wall at the National Museum
      of Women In the Arts,
I paused with awe, first at its size, then texture; it's stunning;
different than printed on the book—there a flat piece of paper
      art, but here,
three-dimensional canvas; paint, carefully applied, leaps, pain
      spirals,
the center reverberates in my eyes. My mind wants to
      comprehend the design,
application of color, this artistic elucidation of a flower; Chicago
      captures
the locus of our strength and power; locates it between our
      legs. Her art arouses.

Encountering the original reminds me what it was like to be
      with a woman
for the first time—how pubic hair felt in my young hand—
      what it was like
to feel the back of a woman's neck, to make her shiver, shake

with my own fingers—

I remember: it is different to experience life than just to imagine
it.

This is what it will be like to be old. Today, I only imagine my
old age: bald pussy,

gray mane, an expanse of empty days, but I'm still bearded
below, brown above,

and busy as buggery; but someday, suddenly, I'll not be
imagining:

age will arrive in my body. I will walk through the flower.

I hope it will be like Judy Chicago's painting: vivid, verberate,
vital.

PLUMBING

When the regulator valve
springs a leak after Thanksgiving,
I turn off the water main
and the hot-water heat.
My wife and I buy gallon jugs
of water, a bushel of wood
to bunker down.

In the chill of our house,
she learns new things about me:
I can wash dishes in a pot
with only a half gallon
of water, heated on the stove,
and wait until we're out
in public for restrooms.

I, too, learn a thing or two.
With small pieces of wood,
large logs, newspaper,
a stack of New Mexican
pinyon, she can stroke
the fire's flames all day long
until I become jealous.

For two days, we cook
elaborate dinners for the benefit
of oven heat. Then, Sunday
evening, amid steaming
vegetables, basting meat,
rising bread, baking brownies,
she looks at me and says,

I miss my mother.
The household chill reminds
her of the world's warmth
when mother was alive.
Now, orphaned at forty-one,
she is in alone our frigid house.
I was just enjoying

this time, waiting
for Monday morning when
the plumber will arrive.
He fixes everything.
For an entire week, our house
smells: pinyon and grief,
the many ways we make love.

CUNTS

For Tee Corinne

Three hours before Tee Corinne died
I was in a grange in Vermont for a poetry reading,
I started with poems about social justice –
what the organizer wanted –
but it was heavy and, dare I say, dour
so I ended with one that had always been
a crowd favorite about sex in my fantasy single life
only I had forgotten that I always read it
to queer audiences and this audience was
definitely not queer and the poem contains
both the "p word" and the "f word"
my wife hadn't forgotten and she,
in the audience, looked on with horror
and even I, as I was reading,
realized the depth of my profanity
and read the poem more slowly thinking
could I change it? change the words?
call it my "love hatch?" insert "making love?"
but those words didn't suit the diction
so I barreled on with "eating my pussy"
and "fucking me real hard" and
when I was done I was exhausted and

{ 56 }

the northeastern audience politely applauded and
I left flush with the power of my tongue and
my friend who was reading next
she had to slink on to the stage and
sit there in the mess of my come
and her mother and sister were there and
I felt bad about showing them all of my stuff
but in the moment, in the moment,
I felt powerful
talking about pussy
as powerful as I had felt three days earlier
when, after making love to my wife,
who was only eight hours away
from the onset of her menses and
had a deep purple lining inside her labia and vagina,
the way our bodies do when they are eager
to slough off the unnecessary lining of our womb
it was so beautiful and she was relaxed
and we were on vacation, so I said
I'd like to take a picture and she said sure and
I did, two actually, although they didn't capture
that deep purple in part because
she was over taken by prudery
at the last moment and
prattled on about this is how people end up
with compromising photographs on the web
or in the news and she made me swear

that I would never show them to anyone and
never, ever put them on the internet,
a promise I easily made
because I knew that I had the photographs,
two of them, showing her pussy, her labia
slightly separated, her clitoris swollen, erect,
I am only telling you this
because three days and three hours later
Tee Corinne died and it was because of her
that I wrote the poem and took those pictures
somehow it seems like a proper homage to her
that while she was dying
all of this was happening.
You should probably know
I have kept my promise to my wife —
no one has seen the pictures of her pussy,
but I look at them every day
and I am happy —
happy for my wife's cunt and
thankful to Tee who enabled me
to see lesbian love and cunts in color.

WAS ELIZABETH BISHOP
A LESBIAN?

The first time I heard this question
the words came from my lips
posed to the professor in the too-hot
classroom of an ivy-covered,
though hopelessly Midwestern, hall;
he looked at me and sighed,
Such things are not relevant to poetry.
What matters is she was a master—
one of the greats of our century.
I spent ten years looking for the answer,
not among poets but lesbians—
as if I might construct my own
hand-made genealogy connecting me
to Miss EB the way Ginsberg articulated
his seminal lineage to Whitman.
Only Ginsberg was more successful,
I was mired in meetings
and more and more things
that took me away from Elizabeth
and Emily and Gertrude—who was
and told, master or not, *lifting belly,*
she said, a *rose is a rose is a rose*—
until eventually I found a way to return,

to sit in this room, student again and
now teacher too, waiting for one young
woman, quite unlike my younger self,
to ask that question again, and the answer,
my answer, will change this whole world.

MAKING LOVE AFTER MANY YEARS

It isn't easy. I can't tell you how many times, young and single,
I thought married sex would be the best—available, reliable,
heck, even guaranteed—in reality, it's not any of these; too
        many nights
we bound into bed with amorous anticipation only to have
our pheromones masked by tryptophan; our sultry eyes turn
from 'come hither' to 'way over yonder,' and we move from sex
        to sleep,
from fantasy to dream, from snickers to snores; this is better,
actually, than evenings our desires are lost to conversation—
quick catch-us-ups on bill paying, family, or other living
        mundanities—
talk is important, of course, especially to sustain a long-term,
committed relationship, but this is the truth: in bed the topic
doesn't matter, words alone encourage the sinister possibilities
that lurk beneath the sheets—exchanges of import with their
        inevitable
disagreements, at best; bickering, at worst—bickering—the all-
        time
mood-killer which is why I understand why, though I'm not yet
        forty,
married people have sex only on the weekends—weekdays are
        filled

with work at home and work at work and even the weekends
       have to be
protected from laborious encroachments and well-meaning
       family and friends,
amid all that, it's amazing that children are ever created let
       alone that adults
have time and energy to recreate in a physical, or sexual nature,
all that to say, this is why, when you take me into your arms
on a particular Thursday night, and we even have a guest in
       the house
and the sheets are somewhat dirty, when you press your lips to
       mine,
let them linger longer than Thursday night usually allows,
       when I am lost
in your tongue, your lips, when you cause me to sigh with an
       unexpectedly
tender caress of my thigh, I am surprised, not shocked, but
       pleased,
because making love after many years isn't always easy.

JULIE R. ENSZER (Saginaw, MI, 1970) has published poems in *Room of One's Own, Long Shot, Feminist Studies, Bridges, So to Speak,* and many other journals. Her essays and columns have been featured *The Washington Blade, Alternet, off our backs,* and the anthology *Second Person Queer.* She worked for many years in the lesbian, gay, bisexual, and transgender movement in the United States including as the director of the gay and lesbian community center in metropolitan Detroit. She completed her undergraduate degree in English and Women's Studies at the University of Michigan and received a MFA in poetry from the University of Maryland in 2008. She lives in University Park, Maryland and is working on her PhD in Women's Studies at the University of Maryland.

A MIDSUMMER NIGHT'S PRESS was founded by Lawrence Schimel in New Haven, CT in 1991. Using a letterpress, it published broadsides of poems by Nancy Willard, Joe Haldeman, and Jane Yolen, among others, in signed, limited editions of 126 copies, numbered 1-100 and lettered A-Z. One of the broadsides— "Will" by Jane Yolen— won a Rhysling Award. In 1993, the publisher moved to New York and the press went on hiatus until 2007, when it began publishing perfect-bound, commercially-printed books under three imprints:

FABULA RASA: devoted to works inspired by mythology, folklore, and fairy tales. The first titles from this imprint are *Fairy Tales for Writers* by Lawrence Schimel and *Fortune's Lover: A Book of Tarot Poems* by Rachel Pollack.

FUNNY BONES: devoted to works of humor and light verse. The first title from this imprint are *The Good-Neighbor Policy,* a murder mystery told in double dactyls by Edgar Award-winner Charles Ardai.

BODY LANGUAGE: devoted to texts exploring questions of gender and sexual identity. The other titles from this imprint are *This is What Happened in Our Other Life,* the first collection of poems from Lambda Literary Award-winner Achy Obejas; *Banalities* by Brane Mozetič, translated from the Slovene by Elizabeta Zargi with Timothy Liu; and *Mute* by Raymond Luczak.